101

Best Jokes Ever

by the readers of Arrow

Illustrations by
Bojan Redzic

Scholastic Canada Ltd.

Toronto New York London Auckland Sydney
Mexico City New Delhi Hong Kong Buenos Aires

Scholastic Canada Ltd.
175 Hillmount Road, Markham, Ontario L6C 1Z7, Canada

Scholastic Inc.
555 Broadway, New York, NY 10012, USA

Scholastic Australia Pty Limited
PO Box 579, Gosford, NSW 2250, Australia

Scholastic New Zealand Limited
Private Bag 94407, Greenmount, Auckland, New Zealand

Scholastic Ltd.
Villiers House, Clarendon Avenue, Leamington Spa,
Warwickshire CV32 5PR, UK

Library and Archives Canada Cataloguing in Publication
101 best jokes ever : jokes submitted by readers of
Arrow Book Club ; Bojan Redzic, illustrator.
ISBN 0-439-96182-3
1. Wit and humor, Juvenile. 2. Wit and humor,
Canadian (English) I. Redzic, Bojan II. Arrow Book Club. III.
Title: One hundred and one best jokes ever.
PS8375.O54 2004   jC818'.60208   C2004-904518-0

6 5 4 3 2 1   Printed in Canada   04 05 06 07 08

Laugh-o-meter

While all of the jokes in 101 Best Jokes Ever are HILARIOUS, we thought we'd rate our favourites. That doesn't mean they're better than the rest — it just means they tickled our funny bones the most!

This joke put HUGE smiles on our faces!

This joke made us burst out in big, belly-rumbling laughter!

This joke made us smile, burst out in belly-rumbling laughter, and roll around on the floor until tears were streaming down our faces!

What do you get when you cross a lake with a leaky boat?

About halfway, if you're lucky!

— **Stacie**

Why is it always cold in a basketball arena?

Because of all the fans.

— **Brenna**

What's worse than finding a worm in your apple?

Finding half a worm in your apple!

— **Siobhan**

What do you call a T. Rex with a cut?

Dino-sore.

— Ali

What did the rocket ship say to the hamburger?

"Hey, it's almost launch time."

— Samantha

Crystal: *Hey, do you guys think a person can tell you what your future holds, just by looking at cards?*

Courtney: *I do — it's fascinating.*

Brenda: *I don't. I think it's weird.*

Erin: *Well, I sure do. My mom took one look at my report card and told me exactly what would happen when my dad got home!*

— Erin

Why was the tomato
blushing?

*Because it saw the salad
dressing!*

— Adam

Father: *How are your grades, son?*

Son: *Oh . . . under water.*

Father: *What do you mean by "under water"?*

Son: *Well, as in, below sea (C) level!*

— Jessie

What did the cat do when he lost his tail?

He went to the re-tail shop.

— Kelsey

What kind of music do rabbits like to listen to?

Hip-hop.

— Ashton

What kind of plants stick to your clothes and belong at the North Pole?

Brrrs!

— **Kathleen**

What do you call a crazy baker?

A dough-NUT!

— **Stephanie**

Where does the watch repair person get parts?

From the second hand store.

— Lisa

Mrs. Plum: *Steven, give me a sentence that is a question.*

Steven: *Why do I always have to answer the hard ones?*

Mrs. Plum: *Good job!*

— Oswaldo

What did the teenage firefly say to the other teenage firefly?

You glow, girl!

— Talia

Why has no one ever spotted a leopard in Canada?

Because leopards already have spots!

— Natalee

What do you get when you cross a porcupine and a turtle?

A slowpoke!

— Rebecca

What runs around a classroom
stealing answers?

A cheetah!

— Allan

Jennifer: *Would you punish someone for something they didn't do?*

Teacher: *Of course not!*

Jennifer: *Thank goodness, because I didn't do my homework.*

— Harjot

Mother Lion: *What are you doing?*

Baby Lion: *I'm chasing a man around a tree.*

Mother Lion: *How often must I tell you not to play with your food?*

— Angie

How do you catch a squirrel?

Climb up a tree and act like a nut!

— Ashley

**Where does a zit have to grow
for you not to worry about it?**

On someone else.

— Sage

**What happened to the cat who
swallowed a ball of wool?**

She had mittens.

— Joseph

What do you call a boomerang that doesn't come back?

A stick.

— Scott

What do you call a bull that sleeps all day?

A bulldozer.

— Kyle

What do you get when you cross a snowman and a vampire?

Frostbite.

— Tanner

What did the tie say to
the hat?

*You go on ahead. I'll just
hang around.*

— Lisa

Why did the car cross
the road?

*Because the chicken was
driving it.*

— Matthew

Where do cows go for vacation?

Bermooda.

— **Nicholas**

A guy who had just lost his job went to the zoo. The zookeeper asked what he was doing and the guy said, "I don't have a job, and I was looking at the animals."

The zookeeper said, "Well, our gorilla died last week, so we need a gorilla. Come back here Monday. We'll put you in a gorilla suit and you can act like a gorilla."

So the guy returned on Monday, and did a really good job of acting like a gorilla. People made faces at him, and he made faces back. The audience really liked him and thought that he was real.

Then the guy went on a rope and started to swing. He was really enjoying it, but he got so carried away that he fell into the lion's cage! The lion ran toward him, so the guy tried to climb up the wall, crying, "HELP! A lion is trying to get me!"

Then the lion grabbed the guy! He was terrified, but then he heard a whisper in his ear. "Be quiet," the lion said, "or the audience will know we're just people in costumes and we'll lose our jobs!"

— Jillian

Prisoner: *It's not my fault!
I was given a name that
was bound to lead me into a
life of crime!*

Judge: *What is your name?*

Prisoner: *Robin Banks!*

— Courtney

What did one plate say to the other plate?

Dinner's on me.

— **Nicole**

One day three little pigs went to a restaurant. The first little pig ordered roast beef, the second ordered a salad and the third ordered water.

For dessert, the first little pig ordered a piece of cake, the second ordered ice cream and the third ordered water.

At the end of dinner, the waitress said to the third little pig, "All you order is water, water, water! How come?"

The third little pig answered, "Because one of us has to go wee wee wee all the way home!"

— Rachel

Why don't matches play baseball?

Because one strike and they're out!

— Krzysztof

One day three vampire bats
came up with a contest to see
who could suck the most blood
in the least amount of time.

The first bat left and came
back ten minutes later with
blood on his teeth.

The other two bats asked how
he had got it, and he answered,
"See that dog over there?"

"Yes," they answered.

He continued, "I sucked its
blood."

The second bat went and came
back twenty minutes later with
his whole mouth full of blood.

The two other bats asked how he had got it, and he answered, "See that cow over there?"

"Yes," they answered.

He continued, "I sucked its blood."

The third bat went and came back five minutes later with his face completely covered in blood.

The other two bats asked how he had got it, and he answered, "See that post over there?"

"Yes," the other two answered.

He continued, "Well, I didn't."

— Gabriel

When was the Great
Depression?

*Last week, when I got my report
card.*

— **Blake**

When did the fly fly?

When the spider spied her!

— **Calum**

How are hockey players and magicians alike?

They both perform hat tricks.

— **Maaz**

Why did the egg go to the jungle?

It was an egg-splorer.

— **Kurt**

What would you do if
a bull charged you?

Pay him cash.

—— Jason

My grandma started walking five miles a day when she was sixty years old.

She's ninety-seven now, and we don't know where the heck she is!

— Maille

Billy: *Have you heard of the skunk with no nose?*

Bobby: *A skunk with no nose? How does it smell?*

Billy: *Awful!*

— Cameron

Principal: *Will you pass the mustard?*

Teacher: *No, I think I'll flunk it.*

— Adam

Why was Cinderella kicked off the basketball team?

She kept running away from the ball!

— Gina

A police officer pulled over
a guy driving a convertible.
The guy had a penguin in the
front seat.

"Is that a real penguin?"
asked the officer.

"Yeah, I just picked it up,"
the guy responded.

"Well, why don't you take
him to the zoo?" said the police
officer.

"Okay," the guy agreed.

But the next week the police
officer saw the man with
the penguin again. "I thought

you said you were going to take
him to the zoo," the police
officer said.

"I did," said the man, "and
we had such a good time, we're
going to a hockey game."

— Nikita

Why did the cereal hide in the cupboard until it was safe to come out?

Because it heard there was a cereal killer on the loose.

— Arthur

A sandwich walks into a coffee shop and asks for a coffee.
    The waitress says, "Sorry, we don't serve food in here."

— Alyssa

A man said to his neighbour, "I just bought a new state-of-the-art hearing aid. It cost me thousands of dollars."

"Really," said the neighbour, "what kind is it?"

"12:30."

— C. J.

How do you stop a herd of elephants from charging?

Take away their credit cards.

— Kyla

"Last night was the most terrible night ever!"

"What happened?"

"I dreamt I ate a fifty-pound marshmallow!"

"What's so bad about that?"

"When I woke up, my pillow was gone!"

— Ryker

Why do elephants never get rich?

Because they work for peanuts.

— Sarah

What did one pig say to the other pig when he found gold in the dirt?

I'm filthy, stinking rich!

— Jason

Teacher: *Brenda, how many fingers do you have?*

Brenda: *Ten.*

Teacher: *Right. Now, if you lost four in an accident, what would you have?*

Brenda: *No more piano lessons.*

— Jasmine

What kind of jokes do smart
kids tell?

Wisecracks!

— Taylor

Five cats were sitting on a fence.
One jumped off. How many
were left?

None — they were all copycats.

— Ashley

A little girl came home from school one day, crying. Her mother asked her what was wrong and the girl replied, "I got punished for something I didn't do."

The mother was angry about this, so she picked up the phone to call her daughter's teacher.

"By the way," she said. "What was it that you didn't do?"

"My homework," replied the girl.

— Brandi-Lee

What do you call it when your dog swallows your clock?

Alarming.

— Jesse

What ten-letter word starts with gas?

Automobile.

— Lucielle

Kid: *Doctor, doctor! Wherever I touch myself it hurts! What's wrong with me?*

Doctor: *You have a broken finger.*

— Ben

Why did the man stare at the can of orange juice?

Because it said concentrate.

— Marsadi

Teacher: *If you were to add 4329 and 7636, multiply the answer by 3 and divide by 7, what would you get?*

Student: *I would get the wrong answer.*

— Hannah

Why did the school bell think it was engaged?

Because someone gave it a ring.

— Amanda

What did the snail say
when he caught a ride on
the turtle's back?

Whoaaa!!

— Chase

Why do bears get married?

Because they love going on honeymoons.

— **Manpreet**

What do witches and candles have in common?

They are both wicked.

— **Zina**

Why did the turkey cross the road?

It was the chicken's day off.

— Alyssa

How does a farmer keep
track of all his cows?

Using a cow-culator!

— Martina

Why is it hard to fool a slug?

Because you can't pull its leg.

— Emma

Why didn't the rocket have a job?

Because it got fired!

— Lane

What do you call a horse that
lives beside you?

Your neigh-bour.

— Emerjade

What did one wall say to the
other wall?

Meet you at the corner.

— Rezan

What do snowmen eat for breakfast?

Frosted Flakes.

— Jacklyn

Why did the student study on the airplane?

To get a higher education!

— Ricky

What is a ghost's favourite food?

Ice scream!

— Christina

What did one lettuce say to the other before they ate?

Lettuce pray.

— Samantha

What did the big egg say
to the little egg?

I'll beat you.

— Jill

What do computer operators eat for a light snack?

Chips!

— Carol

Why did the traffic light turn red?

*Wouldn't you if you had to change
in the middle of the street?*

— Kristy

**What's black, white and
red all over?**

An embarrassed penguin!

— Hannah

Woman in restaurant: *Is there soup on the menu?*

Waiter: *There was, but I wiped it off.*

— Joanna

What do you call a spy in bed?

An undercover cop.

— Cristy

Why did the apple go to the vet?

It wanted to be dewormed.

— **Ada**

What kind of boats do vampires prefer?

Blood vessels!

— **William**

What do you get when you cross a computer and one million mosquitoes?

A gigabite.

— **Marsadi**

What's green and sings?

Elvis Parsley!

— **Andrew**

What candy is always late?

Choco-late!

— Irene

Why wasn't the clock allowed in the library?

It tocked too much.

— Hayley

What's the only room a ghost won't go into?

The living room!

— **Kayley**

First person: *Our dog is just like one of the family.*

Second person: *Who, your Uncle Charlie?*

— **Khalil**

What do you call a pig
that takes karate?

Pork Chop.

— Courtney

Why was the teddy bear so full?

Because he was stuffed!

— Miranda

Why did the man put a knocker on his door?

Because he wanted to win the No Bell Peace Prize.

— Kelvin

Teacher: *Sid, where is the English Channel?*

Sid: *I don't know. We don't have cable.*

— Marikris

Tommy: *Why does your mother always buy maple furniture?*

Billy: *Because she can't find chocolate or vanilla.*

— Kayla

Why didn't the fireplace go to school?

Because it has the flu!

— Sara

Why do grade fives get different book orders than grade ones?

Because nobody wants grade ones to have Goosebumps!

— Shane

What do you call a boat that
never knocks on doors?

A barge.

— **Chris**

A chicken walks into a bookstore and says, "Book, book," so the clerk gives him a book.

This happens again every day for three days, until the clerk decides he needs to know what the chicken is doing with the books.

He follows the chicken into the forest and watches as it drops the book in front of a frog.

"Book, book," it says.

And the frog replies, "Read it. Read it."

— Harry

Can February March?

No, but April May.

— Michael

What did the sea say to the iceberg?

Nothing. It just waved.

— Mary Rose

Teacher: *Give me a sentence using the word "indisposition."*

Pupil: *I always play centre in hockey because I love playing in-dis-position.*

— **Kageepan**

Why should you never tell secrets in the produce section?

Because the potatoes have eyes, the corn have ears and the beans stalk.

— Wintta